I0703275

REPUBLICANS NERVOUS : ON KAMALA'S RUNNING MATE CHOICE

The Impact of Pennsylvania Governor Josh Shapiro on the 2024 Election

BY: JIM K. CLARK

Copyright © JIM K. CLARK 2024.

All rights reserved. No part of this book may be reproduced, distributed, or transmitted in any form or by any means, including photocopying, recording, or other electronic or mechanical methods, without the prior written permission of the publisher, except in the case of brief quotations embodied in critical reviews and certain other noncommercial uses permitted by copyright law.

DEDICATION

To those who believe in the power of informed choice
and the strength of democratic engagement,

This book is dedicated to the countless individuals who
tirelessly work to understand the complexities of our
political landscape. Your commitment to knowledge,
your passion for justice, and your unwavering dedication
to making a difference inspire us all.

To my family and friends, whose support and
encouragement have been my greatest strength, and to
every reader who seeks to grasp the intricacies of our
political world this book is for you.

May it provide clarity, insight, and inspiration as we
navigate the ever changes of our political journey
together.

With deepest gratitude,

Jim k. Clark

TABLE OF CONTENTS

10. **Bonus**

•Insights from Political Experts on Josh Shapiro's Impact

•Expert Commentary on Shapiro's Candidacy

• Republican Strategists' Views

• Media Analysis on Shapiro's Influence

• Public Opinion and Polling Data

• Future Implications and Predictions

• Case Studies on Vice Presidential Influence

• Strategies for Republicans Moving Forward

• The Role of Social Media

INTRODUCTION

Overview of Kamala Harris's Vice Presidential Candidacy

Kamala Harris, the first female, first Black, and first South Asian Vice President of the United States, has brought a new energy to American politics. Her diverse background as a former prosecutor, California Attorney General, and U.S. Senator has made her a prominent figure in the Biden administration. Harris's candidacy symbolises a progressive shift and aims to address critical issues like criminal justice reform, healthcare, and racial equality. As the potential Vice Presidential running mate in the 2024 election, her influence and decisions are under close scrutiny, especially her choice of running mate.

The Significance of Vice Presidential Picks in Elections

Choosing a Vice Presidential running mate is a crucial decision in any election. The right pick can balance the ticket, and a wrong pick can also affect the ticket, appeal to broader voter demographics, to strengthen the overall campaign strategy. A well chosen running mate can attract key swing voters, address the concerns of different voter groups, and even sway the outcome of the election. In Kamala Harris's case, the prospect of selecting Pennsylvania Governor Josh Shapiro as her running mate has particularly made Republicans nervous. His popularity and influence in a key swing state like Pennsylvania could significantly impact the election dynamics and challenge the Republican campaign.

JOSH SHAPIRO: A RISING POLITICAL STAR

Early Life and Career

Josh Shapiro was born on June 20, 1973, in Kansas City, Missouri, and grew up in Montgomery County, Pennsylvania. From his young age, Shapiro demonstrated a keen interest in public service and leadership. He attended the University of Rochester, where he earned a bachelor's degree in political science. During his time in college, he was deeply involved in student government and campus activities, laying the foundation for his future in politics.

After college, Shapiro pursued a law degree from Georgetown University Law Center. His legal education equipped him with the skills and knowledge necessary for a career in public service. Shapiro began his professional journey as a legislative assistant in Washington, D.C., where he worked for U.S. Senator Carl Levin and U.S. Representative Peter Deutsch. This experience in the nation's capital provided him with valuable insights into the legislative process and the workings of the federal government.

Rise to Prominence in Pennsylvania

Shapiro's political career took off when he returned to Pennsylvania and ran for the Pennsylvania House of Representatives. **In 2004,** he was elected to represent the 153rd district, serving the people of Montgomery County. During his tenure, Shapiro earned a reputation as a pragmatic and effective lawmaker. He focused on issues such as healthcare, education, and environmental protection, gaining respect from both colleagues and constituents.

In 2011, Shapiro's career took a significant leap forward when he was elected as a Montgomery County Commissioner. In this role, he demonstrated his ability to lead and manage complex governmental operations. Shapiro's leadership was instrumental in stabilising the county's finances, reducing debt, and increasing transparency. His work as a commissioner showcased his dedication to good governance and fiscal responsibility.

Shapiro's success in local government paved the way for his next big move: running for Pennsylvania Attorney General. In 2016, he won the election and assumed office in January 2017. As Attorney General, Shapiro took on a wide range of issues, from consumer protection and environmental enforcement to combating the opioid crisis and defending civil rights. His tenure was marked by high-profile cases and significant achievements that solidified his standing as a rising star in Pennsylvania politics.

Key Achievements and Controversies

As Pennsylvania's Attorney General, Josh Shapiro has accomplished several notable achievements that have garnered both praise and criticism. One of his most significant accomplishments was his role in the investigation of the Catholic Church's handling of child sexual abuse cases. Shapiro's office released a groundbreaking grand jury report in 2018 that detailed decades of abuse by clergy members and cover-ups by the church officials. This report had a profound impact, leading to legislative changes and increased awareness of the issue nationwide.

Shapiro also played a crucial role in addressing the opioid crisis in Pennsylvania. He took legal action against pharmaceutical companies for their role in fueling the epidemic, securing significant settlements that were used to fund addiction treatment and prevention programs. His efforts in this area demonstrated his commitment to holding powerful entities accountable and advocating for public health.

In addition to these high-profile cases, Shapiro has been a staunch advocate for consumer protection. He has taken on predatory lenders, scam artists, and companies engaging in deceptive practices. His office has secured millions of dollars in restitution for consumers and worked to ensure fair treatment for all Pennsylvanians.

Despite his many achievements, Shapiro's tenure as Attorney General has not been without controversy. Some critics have accused him of being overly ambitious and using his office as a stepping stone for higher political aspirations. They argue that his pursuit of high-profile cases is motivated by a desire for media attention and political gain. However, Shapiro's supporters contend that his actions are driven by a genuine commitment to justice and public service.

Another area of contention has been his stance on certain law enforcement issues. While Shapiro has advocated for criminal justice reform and police accountability, some law enforcement groups have criticised his approach. They argue that his policies could undermine the ability of police officers to effectively do their jobs. Shapiro, however, maintains that his goal is to balance the need for public safety with the need for transparency and accountability.

As Josh Shapiro continues to make headlines and build his political career, his potential selection as Kamala Harris's running mate in the 2024 election has garnered significant attention. His track record of achievements, combined with his ability to navigate complex political landscapes, makes him a compelling choice. For Republicans, the prospect of Shapiro on the ticket presents a formidable challenge, particularly in a key swing state like Pennsylvania.

 Josh Shapiro's journey from a young political enthusiast to a prominent figure in Pennsylvania politics is a testament to his dedication, skill, and determination. His early life and career laid the groundwork for his rise to prominence, and his tenure as Attorney General has been marked by significant achievements and some controversies. As the 2024 election approaches, Shapiro's potential role as Kamala Harris's running mate is poised to shape the political landscape in profound ways.

THE REPUBLICAN RESPONSE

Initial Reactions to Shapiro's Potential Selection

When news broke that Pennsylvania Governor Josh Shapiro might be Kamala Harris's running mate for the 2024 election, it sent ripples through the Republican Party. Many prominent Republican politicians and strategists expressed immediate concern. Shapiro's track record in Pennsylvania, a crucial swing state, posed a significant challenge to their election strategies. His popularity and proven ability to win in a battleground state were seen as major threats.

Prominent Republicans were quick to voice their apprehensions. Senate Minority Leader Mitch McConnell highlighted the potential impact of Shapiro's candidacy on the electoral map, calling him a "formidable opponent." Conservative commentators and media outlets echoed these sentiments, emphasising Shapiro's ability to energise the Democratic base and attract moderate and independent voters.

Key Republican Concerns and Criticisms

Republicans have several specific concerns regarding Shapiro's potential selection as the Democratic vice-presidential candidate. First and foremost, they worry about his appeal to key voter demographics. Shapiro's strong track record in Pennsylvania, a state that played a pivotal role in recent elections, makes him a particularly attractive candidate. His ability to connect with suburban voters, working class families, and minority communities poses a direct threat to Republican efforts to reclaim those votes.

Another major concern is Shapiro's stance on various issues that resonate with a broad spectrum of voters. His work on consumer protection, healthcare, and environmental issues aligns with the priorities of many Americans. Republicans fear that his policy positions and accomplishments could sway voters who are on the fence, particularly in critical swing states.

Criticism of Shapiro also centres on his perceived ambition and political manoeuvring. Some Republicans argue that his high-profile cases and public actions as Attorney General and Governor were motivated more by a desire for media attention and higher office than by genuine public service. They point to his aggressive pursuit of cases against powerful entities and individuals as evidence of his willingness to use his office for personal political gain.

Additionally, Shapiro's approach to law enforcement and criminal justice reform has drawn criticism from some conservative circles. While he advocates for police accountability and criminal justice reform, some Republicans argue that his policies could undermine public safety and law enforcement effectiveness. They contend that his positions on these issues may not sit well with voters who prioritise law and order.

Strategic Shifts in Republican Campaigns

In response to the potential threat posed by Josh Shapiro's selection, Republicans are making several strategic adjustments to their campaigns. Recognizing the need to counter his appeal, they are refining their messaging and policy proposals to better resonate with voters in swing states like Pennsylvania.

One key strategy involves emphasising contrasts between Republican and Democratic policies. Republicans are focusing on economic issues, arguing that their approach to taxation, regulation, and job creation is more beneficial for working-class families. By highlighting differences in economic policy, they aim to appeal to voters who may be swayed by pocketbook issues.

Another strategic shift involves strengthening grassroots efforts and voter outreach. Republicans are ramping up their presence in communities where Shapiro has strong support, particularly in suburban and urban areas. They are investing in targeted advertising, community engagement, and voter mobilisation efforts to ensure their message reaches a broader audience.

Republicans are also working to build new alliances and coalitions to counter Shapiro's influence. They are reaching out to moderate and independent voters, as well as traditionally Democratic constituencies, with tailored messages that address their specific concerns. By broadening their appeal and forming new partnerships, Republicans hope to mitigate Shapiro's impact and gain an edge in critical swing states.

In addition to these efforts, Republicans are preparing to scrutinise Shapiro's record and highlight any perceived weaknesses or controversies. They are digging into his past actions and decisions as Attorney General and Governor, looking for areas where they can challenge his credibility and effectiveness. By focusing on any perceived flaws, they aim to weaken his appeal and cast doubt on his suitability as a vice-presidential candidate.

The prospect of Josh Shapiro as Kamala Harris's running mate has undoubtedly made Republicans nervous. His popularity, track record, and policy positions present significant challenges to their campaign strategies. In response, Republicans are making strategic shifts to counter his appeal, emphasising policy contrasts, strengthening grassroots efforts, and building new alliances. As the 2024 election approaches, the battle for key swing states like

Pennsylvania will be intense, with both parties vying to sway voters and secure victory.

IMPACT ON SWING STATES

Pennsylvania's Crucial Role in the 2024 Election

Pennsylvania has long been a pivotal swing state in American elections. Its diverse demographic landscape, which includes a mix of urban, suburban, and rural voters, makes it a microcosm of the broader national electorate. The state's 20 electoral votes are highly coveted by both major parties, often serving as a bellwether for the overall election outcome.

In recent elections, Pennsylvania has been known for its tight margins and shifting political dynamics. For example, in the 2020 presidential election, Joe Biden narrowly won Pennsylvania, securing its electoral votes by less than a percentage point. This close contest underscores the importance of Pennsylvania in determining the final results of national elections.

With Kamala Harris potentially selecting Josh Shapiro as her running mate, Pennsylvania's significance in the 2024 election becomes even more pronounced. Shapiro, as the current Governor of Pennsylvania, has deep connections with the state's electorate and a strong understanding of its political landscape. His presence on the ticket could further solidify the Democratic hold on Pennsylvania or sway undecided voters.

Shapiro's Influence in Other Swing States

Josh Shapiro's influence is not confined to Pennsylvania alone. His reputation and political clout could extend to other key swing states, amplifying his impact on the national stage. Shapiro's record as Attorney General and Governor highlights his ability to address pressing issues such as healthcare, criminal justice, and consumer protection topics that resonate with voters across various states.

Shapiro's potential role as Kamala Harris's running mate might enhance the Democratic ticket's appeal in other swing states by drawing attention to his accomplishments and positions on critical issues. His reputation for effective governance and his pragmatic approach to problem-solving could attract voters in states like Michigan, Wisconsin, and Ohio, where similar issues are at the forefront of electoral concerns.

 Shapiro's political strategy and campaign style could serve as a model for Democratic candidates in other battleground states. His ability to connect with diverse voter groups and his successful track record in Pennsylvania might offer valuable insights and strategies for Democrats aiming to secure victories in other competitive regions.

Potential Shifts in Electoral Dynamics

The potential selection of Josh Shapiro as Kamala Harris's running mate could lead to significant shifts in electoral dynamics. Shapiro's candidacy could influence voter behaviour and campaign strategies in several ways:

1. Increased Democratic Engagement: Shapiro's presence on the ticket could energise Democratic voters, particularly in Pennsylvania. His strong ties to the state and his reputation for effective leadership might mobilise voters who previously felt disconnected or disengaged from the political process.

2. Impact on Republican Strategies: Republicans may need to reassess their approach in response to Shapiro's candidacy. His appeal and influence in swing states could force Republicans to adapt their messaging and campaign strategies to counter his impact effectively. This might include intensifying efforts in Pennsylvania and other key states or shifting focus to different voter demographics.

3. Shifts in Voter Priorities: Shapiro's policy positions and achievements could shift the focus of electoral debates. Voters in swing states might place greater emphasis on issues that Shapiro highlights, such as healthcare reform or consumer protection. This could

lead to changes in campaign messaging and strategy by
both parties.

4. Potential for New Alliances: Shapiro's candidacy
might lead to the formation of new political alliances and
coalitions. His appeal to moderate and independent
voters could encourage Democrats to forge partnerships
with local leaders and organisations in other swing
states, broadening their support base and increasing
their chances of success.

5. Electoral Map Changes: Depending on Shapiro's
influence and the effectiveness of his campaign, there
could be shifts in the electoral map. States that were
previously considered strongholds for one party might
become more competitive, altering the overall dynamics
of the 2024 election.

Josh Shapiro's potential role as Kamala Harris's running
mate is poised to have a profound impact on the 2024
election, particularly in key swing states like
Pennsylvania. His influence could extend beyond his
home state, affecting voter behaviour and campaign
strategies across the nation. As the election
approaches, the shifts in electoral dynamics will be
closely watched, with both parties adapting their
strategies to address the challenges and opportunities
presented by Shapiro's candidacy.

PUBLIC PERCEPTION AND MEDIA COVERAGE

How the Media Portrays Josh Shapiro

Josh Shapiro's media portrayal is multifaceted, reflecting both his accomplishments and the controversies surrounding him. Generally, the media depicts Shapiro as a skilled and effective leader with a solid track record in Pennsylvania. His tenure as Attorney General and Governor is often highlighted, showcasing his efforts in addressing high-profile issues such as consumer protection, the opioid crisis, and child abuse investigations.

Positive media coverage emphasizes Shapiro's role in leading significant legal actions against powerful entities, such as the Catholic Church in the child sexual abuse scandal. This coverage portrays him as a principled advocate for justice, highlighting his dedication to public service and his ability to tackle complex and sensitive issues.

Conversely, some media outlets have scrutinised Shapiro's political ambitions and strategies. Critics argue that his high-profile actions and public statements are driven more by a desire for personal gain and media attention than by genuine concern for public issues. This portrayal suggests that Shapiro's actions may be strategically motivated, positioning him as a savvy political operator rather than just a dedicated public servant.

Public Opinion Trends and Polls

Public opinion on Josh Shapiro is generally favourable, reflecting his successful governance and high-profile achievements. Polls show that Shapiro enjoys significant support in Pennsylvania, where his approval ratings have been relatively strong throughout his career. His reputation for addressing key issues like the opioid epidemic and consumer protection has resonated with many voters, contributing to his positive image.

However, Shapiro's potential selection as Kamala Harris's running mate introduces a new dynamic to public opinion. Polls indicate that his presence on the ticket could significantly influence voter preferences. In Pennsylvania, Shapiro's candidacy is seen as a potential asset for the Democratic ticket, as he is well-regarded and has a strong track record in the state.

Nationally, Shapiro's impact is more mixed. While he is respected for his accomplishments, his potential role as a vice-presidential candidate may not yet fully resonate with voters outside Pennsylvania. Polls suggest that while Shapiro could energise the Democratic base and appeal to moderate voters, his influence on undecided voters and independents is still evolving.

Influence on Swing Voters and Independents

Josh Shapiro's candidacy could play a crucial role in shaping the opinions of swing voters and independents, who are often decisive in elections. His record as Governor and Attorney General provides a strong foundation for appealing to these key voter groups.

Swing voters, who are known for being more open to different political perspectives and less committed to one party, may find Shapiro's pragmatic approach and achievements appealing. His focus on practical issues such as healthcare reform, consumer protection, and criminal justice could resonate with voters who prioritise effective governance over partisan politics.

Shapiro's ability to connect with independents is also significant. His reputation for tackling high-profile cases and addressing critical issues may align with the concerns of independent voters who are looking for a candidate with a proven record of problem solving. His potential role as Kamala Harris's running mate could enhance the appeal of the Democratic ticket to these voters, particularly if he is able to effectively communicate his policy positions and vision for the future.

Additionally, Shapiro's influence on swing voters could be bolstered by his strategic focus on key battleground states. His experience and understanding of the political landscape in Pennsylvania, along with his ability to address issues that matter to voters, could make him a compelling candidate for those in pivotal states.

Josh Shapiro's media portrayal and public opinion reflect a combination of respect for his accomplishments and scrutiny of his political strategies. His potential role as Kamala Harris's running mate has the potential to impact voter perceptions significantly, particularly among swing voters and independents. As the 2024 election approaches, Shapiro's influence will likely continue to evolve, shaping the dynamics of the campaign and the broader electoral landscape.

REPUBLICAN STRATEGIES MOVING FORWARD

Changes in Messaging and Campaign Focus

In response to the potential selection of Josh Shapiro as Kamala Harris's running mate, Republicans are recalibrating their messaging and campaign focus to address the new dynamics of the 2024 election. Shapiro's strong standing in Pennsylvania and his reputation as a formidable political figure prompt Republicans to adjust their strategies to counteract his influence effectively.

One key change in Republican messaging involves sharpening their focus on economic issues. Recognizing Shapiro's appeal on issues like consumer protection and healthcare, Republicans are emphasising their own economic policies, particularly those related to tax cuts, deregulation, and job creation. By highlighting their approach to economic growth and fiscal responsibility, Republicans aim to differentiate themselves from the Democratic ticket and appeal to voters concerned about economic stability and prosperity.

Additionally, Republicans are concentrating on portraying Shapiro as a typical politician driven by political ambition. They are framing his high-profile legal cases and public actions as attempts to gain media attention rather than genuine efforts to address public concerns. This narrative aims to cast doubt on Shapiro's authenticity and effectiveness, positioning Republicans as the more reliable and principled choice.

Adjustments in Policy Proposals

To counter Shapiro's potential influence and appeal, Republicans are also revising their policy proposals to better resonate with voters in key swing states. Shifts in policy focus include:

1. Economic Policy: Republicans are placing renewed emphasis on their economic platform, advocating for tax reforms, lower regulation, and incentives for businesses to drive economic growth. This approach seeks to appeal to voters who prioritise economic stability and job creation, countering Shapiro's emphasis on consumer protection and healthcare.

2. Healthcare: Given Shapiro's work on healthcare issues, Republicans are refining their healthcare proposals to present a strong alternative. They are promoting their plans for reducing healthcare costs, expanding access, and improving the efficiency of the healthcare system. By offering clear and compelling healthcare solutions, Republicans aim to address voter concerns and differentiate themselves from the Democratic ticket.

3. Criminal Justice Reform: Shapiro's record on criminal justice reform, Republicans are emphasising their commitment to law and order. They are advocating for policies that support law enforcement, enhance public safety, and address issues related to crime and violence. This focus aims to appeal to voters who prioritise a tough-on-crime stance and are concerned about potential disruptions to public safety.

New Republican Alliances and Tactics

Addition to changes in messaging and policy proposals, Republicans are forming new alliances and adopting tactics to strengthen their campaign efforts:

1. Building Coalitions: Republicans are forging alliances with local leaders, business groups, and community organisations in key battleground states. These partnerships aim to enhance grassroots support and mobilise voters who may be swayed by Shapiro's candidacy. By collaborating with influential figures and organisations, Republicans seek to broaden their appeal and increase their chances of success in crucial swing states.

2. Targeted Advertising: To effectively counter Shapiro's influence, Republicans are investing in targeted advertising campaigns. These campaigns are designed to reach specific voter demographics in swing states, highlighting key policy differences and emphasising Republican strengths. By utilising data-driven strategies and micro-targeting, Republicans aim to maximise their impact and sway undecided voters.

3. Enhanced Voter Outreach: Republicans are ramping up their voter outreach efforts, focusing on engaging with voters in communities where Shapiro's appeal is strong. This includes door-to-door canvassing, phone banking, and digital outreach to ensure their message reaches a broad audience. By engaging directly with voters and addressing their concerns, Republicans aim to build support and counter Shapiro's influence.

4. Debate and Media Strategy: Republicans are preparing for potential debates and media appearances by developing strategies to effectively challenge Shapiro's record and policy positions. They are equipping their candidates with talking points and counterarguments to address Shapiro's strengths and vulnerabilities. This preparation is aimed at making a strong case to voters and reinforcing the Republican platform.

As Josh Shapiro's potential selection as Kamala Harris's running mate reshapes the 2024 electoral landscape, Republicans are adapting their strategies to address the new challenges and opportunities. By refining their messaging, adjusting policy proposals, forming new alliances, and implementing targeted tactics, Republicans aim to counter Shapiro's influence and strengthen their position in the election. The evolving strategies reflect the dynamic nature of the campaign and the critical importance of key swing states in determining the outcome of the 2024 presidential race.

HISTORICAL COMPARISONS

Vice Presidential Picks That Shaped Elections

The choice of a vice presidential running mate has often played a pivotal role in shaping presidential elections. Historically, vice presidential picks have impacted electoral dynamics, influenced campaign strategies, and occasionally altered the course of the election. A few notable examples highlight how these selections have shaped American political history:

1. Lyndon B. Johnson (1960): When John F. Kennedy chose Lyndon B. Johnson as his running mate in 1960, it was a strategic move designed to balance the ticket. Johnson, a seasoned Senate leader from Texas, helped Kennedy secure crucial support in the South, a region where the Democratic Party had traditionally been strong but was facing internal challenges. Johnson's presence on the ticket bolstered Kennedy's appeal in Southern states, contributing to his narrow victory over Richard Nixon.

2. George H. W. Bush (1980): Ronald Reagan's choice of George H. W. Bush as his running mate in

1980 was a significant factor in his campaign's success. Bush, a former CIA Director and Texas Congressman, brought a wealth of experience and credibility to the ticket. His selection helped reassure moderate Republicans and independents who were concerned about Reagan's conservative positions. Bush's role as a unifying figure played a crucial part in Reagan's landslide victory over Jimmy Carter.

3. Sarah Palin (2008): John McCain's selection of Sarah Palin as his running mate in 2008 was a dramatic and controversial choice. Palin, then the Governor of Alaska, energised the Republican base with her populist appeal and fresh perspective. However, her lack of experience and controversial statements also led to significant scrutiny and debate. While Palin's selection brought enthusiasm to McCain's campaign, it did not ultimately prevent Barack Obama from winning the presidency.

4. Joe Biden (2008): Barack Obama's selection of Joe Biden as his vice-presidential running mate in 2008 was a strategic move designed to bring experience and foreign policy expertise to the ticket. Biden's long tenure in the Senate and his reputation as a seasoned statesman helped complement Obama's profile as a relatively inexperienced senator. Biden's selection was instrumental in building a broad coalition of voters, contributing to Obama's victory over John McCain.

Lessons from Previous Republican and Democratic Choices

Examining past vice-presidential selections provides valuable insights into how these choices can impact elections:

1. Balancing the Ticket: One of the key lessons from historical vice-presidential picks is the importance of balancing the ticket. Candidates are often chosen to complement the presidential nominee by addressing perceived weaknesses or appealing to different voter demographics. For example, Johnson balanced Kennedy's youthful image with his own political experience, while Biden provided foreign policy expertise to complement Obama's background.

2. Influencing Swing States: Vice-presidential choices can influence key swing states and regions. Selecting a running mate with strong ties to important electoral battlegrounds can enhance a ticket's appeal in those areas. Reagan's choice of Bush helped secure Texas, while Kennedy's selection of Johnson bolstered support in the South. Understanding regional dynamics and selecting a running mate who resonates with voters in crucial states can be a strategic advantage.

3. Energising the Base: A vice-presidential pick can energise a party's base and mobilise supporters. Palin's selection, for example, invigorated the Republican base with her populist appeal. Conversely, candidates who do not align well with the party's core supporters or fail to inspire enthusiasm can face challenges. A successful pick should resonate with the party's base while also appealing to a broader electorate.

4. Managing Controversies: The impact of vice-presidential choices can be influenced by how well candidates manage controversies and media scrutiny. Palin's selection faced significant challenges due to her controversial statements and perceived lack of experience. Effective communication and handling of controversies are essential for maintaining a positive image and avoiding negative distractions during the campaign.

5. Complementing the Presidential Nominee: The vice-presidential candidate should complement the presidential nominee by bringing strengths and qualities that enhance the overall ticket. Biden's experience and credibility helped address concerns about Obama's inexperience, while Bush's background provided reassurance to moderate Republicans. A successful pick should contribute to a cohesive and effective campaign strategy.

Vice presidential picks have historically played a significant role in shaping presidential elections by influencing voter perceptions, balancing the ticket, and impacting key swing states. The lessons from past choices highlight the importance of strategic decision-making in selecting a running mate who complements the presidential candidate, energises the base, and addresses key campaign challenges. As the 2024 election approaches, the selection of a vice-presidential candidate will continue to be a critical factor in shaping the electoral landscape and determining the outcome of the race.

HISTORICAL COMPARISONS

Vice Presidential Picks That Shaped Elections

The choice of a vice presidential running mate has often played a pivotal role in shaping presidential elections. Historically, vice-presidential picks have impacted electoral dynamics, influenced campaign strategies, and occasionally altered the course of the election. A few notable examples highlight how these selections have shaped American political history:

1. Lyndon B. Johnson (1960): When John F. Kennedy choose Lyndon B. Johnson as his running mate in 1960, it was a strategic move designed to balance the ticket. Johnson, a seasoned Senate leader from Texas, helped Kennedy secure crucial support in the South, a region where the Democratic Party had traditionally been strong but was facing internal challenges. Johnson's presence on the ticket bolstered Kennedy's appeal in Southern states, contributing to his narrow victory over Richard Nixon.

2. George H. W. Bush (1980): Ronald Reagan's choice of George H. W. Bush as his running mate in 1980 was a significant factor in his campaign's success. Bush, a former CIA Director and Texas Congressman, brought a wealth of experience and credibility to the ticket. His selection helped reassure moderate Republicans and independents who were concerned about Reagan's conservative positions. Bush's role as a unifying figure played a crucial part in Reagan's landslide victory over Jimmy Carter.

3. Sarah Palin (2008): John McCain's selection of Sarah Palin as his running mate in 2008 was a dramatic and controversial choice. Palin, then the Governor of Alaska, energised the Republican base with her populist appeal and fresh perspective. However, her lack of experience and controversial statements also led to significant scrutiny and debate. While Palin's selection brought enthusiasm to McCain's campaign, it did not ultimately prevent Barack Obama from winning the presidency.

4. Joe Biden (2008): Barack Obama's selection of Joe Biden as his vice-presidential running mate in 2008 was a strategic move designed to bring experience and foreign policy expertise to the ticket. Biden's long tenure in the Senate and his reputation as a seasoned statesman helped complement Obama's profile as a relatively inexperienced senator. Biden's selection was instrumental in building a broad coalition of voters, contributing to Obama's victory over John McCain.

Lessons from Previous Republican and Democratic Choices

Examining past vice-presidential selections provides valuable insights into how these choices can impact elections:

1. Balancing the Ticket: One of the key lessons from historical vice-presidential picks is the importance of balancing the ticket. Candidates are often chosen to complement the presidential nominee by addressing perceived weaknesses or appealing to different voter demographics. For example, Johnson balanced Kennedy's youthful image with his own political experience, while Biden provided foreign policy expertise to complement Obama's background.

2. Influencing Swing States: Vice presidential choices can influence key swing states and regions. Selecting a running mate with strong ties to important electoral battlegrounds can enhance a ticket's appeal in those areas. Reagan's choice of Bush helped secure Texas, while Kennedy's selection of Johnson bolstered support in the South. Understanding regional dynamics and selecting a running mate who resonates with voters in crucial states can be a strategic advantage.

3. Energising the Base: A vice-presidential pick can energise a party's base and mobilise supporters. Palin's selection, for example, invigorated the Republican base with her populist appeal. Conversely, candidates who do not align well with the party's core supporters or fail to inspire enthusiasm can face challenges. A successful pick should resonate with the party's base while also appealing to a broader electorate.

4. Managing Controversies: The impact of vice-presidential choices can be influenced by how well candidates manage controversies and media scrutiny. Palin's selection faced significant challenges due to her controversial statements and perceived lack of experience. Effective communication and handling of controversies are essential for maintaining a positive image and avoiding negative distractions during the campaign.

5. Complementing the Presidential Nominee: The vice-presidential candidate should complement the presidential nominee by bringing strengths and qualities that enhance the overall ticket. Biden's experience and credibility helped address concerns about Obama's inexperience, while Bush's background provided reassurance to moderate Republicans. A successful pick should contribute to a cohesive and effective campaign strategy.

Vice presidential picks have historically played a significant role in shaping presidential elections by influencing voter perceptions, balancing the ticket, and impacting key swing states. The lessons from past choices highlight the importance of strategic decision-making in selecting a running mate who complements the presidential candidate, energises the base, and addresses key campaign challenges. As the 2024 election approaches, the selection of a vice-presidential candidate will continue to be a critical factor in shaping the electoral landscape and determining the outcome of the race.

CONCLUSION

Summary of Key Points

In examining the potential impact of Josh Shapiro's selection as Kamala Harris's running mate, several key points emerge:

1. Political Profile of Josh Shapiro: Shapiro's rise as a prominent political figure in Pennsylvania, from his early career to his current role as Governor, highlights his significant influence. His achievements in addressing major issues like consumer protection and criminal justice reform have established him as a formidable player in both state and national politics.

2. Republican Response: The Republican reaction to Shapiro's potential selection has been multifaceted. Initial responses include concerns about Shapiro's influence in Pennsylvania and other swing states. Republicans are adjusting their campaign strategies to counteract his appeal, focusing on economic issues, healthcare, and law enforcement, while also forming new alliances and refining their outreach tactics.

3. Impact on Swing States: Shapiro's potential role could significantly impact key swing states, especially Pennsylvania. His presence on the ticket may enhance Democratic prospects in these states and influence voter behaviour. Republicans are responding by recalibrating their strategies to address these shifts and mitigate Shapiro's influence.

4. Media Coverage and Public Perception: Media portrayals of Shapiro reflect both admiration for his achievements and scrutiny of his political motives. Public opinion trends indicate a generally favourable view of Shapiro in Pennsylvania, with his potential influence extending to other swing states. His ability to appeal to independents and swing voters is a crucial factor in the evolving electoral dynamics.

5. Historical Comparisons: Historical vice-presidential picks that have shaped elections reveal the strategic importance of selecting a running mate who can balance the ticket, influence swing states, energise the base, and complement the presidential nominee. Lessons from past choices underscore the impact of these decisions on electoral outcomes.

Final Thoughts on Shapiro's Influence on Republican Politics

Josh Shapiro's potential selection as Kamala Harris's running mate introduces a significant variable into the

2024 presidential race. His established reputation, political achievements, and strategic positioning in Pennsylvania make him a notable factor in the electoral landscape. The Republican Party's response to this potential choice reflects the importance of addressing new challenges and opportunities presented by Shapiro's influence.

As Shapiro continues to shape the narrative of the campaign, his impact on Republican politics will likely be substantial. His ability to mobilise voters, influence swing states, and alter campaign strategies highlights the critical role of vice-presidential selections in modern elections. For Republicans, adapting to Shapiro's potential influence will be essential in crafting an effective strategy to compete in the increasingly complex and competitive 2024 race.

Ultimately, Shapiro's candidacy could reshape the dynamics of the election, prompting both parties to refine their approaches and respond to the evolving political landscape. As the campaign progresses, the interplay between Shapiro's influence and the Republican strategies will be a key factor in determining the outcome of the 2024 presidential election.

BONUSES

INSIGHTS FROM POLITICAL EXPERTS ON JOSH SHAPIRO'S IMPACT

Expert Commentary on Shapiro's Candidacy

Political experts have offered a range of perspectives on Josh Shapiro's potential impact as Kamala Harris's running mate. Analysts praise Shapiro for his strong political credentials and strategic importance in Pennsylvania. His record as Governor and Attorney General showcases his ability to handle high-profile issues and connect with a broad electorate. Experts argue that his inclusion on the ticket could bolster the Democratic campaign by solidifying support in a crucial swing state and appealing to moderate and independent voters.

Republican Strategists' Views

Republican strategists have expressed concerns about Shapiro's influence. They highlight his strong performance in Pennsylvania and his potential to sway undecided voters in key swing states. Strategists are wary of Shapiro's appeal to moderates and independents and are adapting their campaign strategies accordingly. They emphasise the need to counter Shapiro's strengths by focusing on their own policy achievements and addressing the key issues he champions, such as healthcare and criminal justice reform.

Media Analysis on Shapiro's Influence

Media analysis of Shapiro's potential role focuses on his ability to impact the electoral landscape. Coverage often highlights his achievements and his strategic importance in Pennsylvania. Media outlets discuss how Shapiro's candidacy might affect voter perceptions and campaign dynamics. While some reports emphasise his positive attributes and potential to energise the Democratic base, others scrutinise his political ambitions and the implications of his selection for the broader election strategy.

Public Opinion and Polling Data

Polling data reveal mixed but generally favourable views of Shapiro. In Pennsylvania, Shapiro's approval ratings are strong, reflecting his successful governance and popularity. Nationally, opinion is more divided, with some voters viewing Shapiro as a competent and appealing candidate, while others are less convinced. Polls suggest that Shapiro's presence on the ticket could influence key swing states and impact the overall electoral dynamics, with potential to shift voter preferences in favour of the Democratic ticket.

Future Implications and Predictions

Looking ahead, Shapiro's impact on the 2024 election could be significant. Experts predict that his candidacy might enhance Democratic chances in Pennsylvania and other swing states. The Republican response will be crucial in shaping the election's outcome, as they adapt their strategies to counter Shapiro's influence. The evolving dynamics will likely result in a highly competitive race, with both parties refining their approaches based on Shapiro's role and the broader political landscape.

Case Studies on Vice Presidential Influence

Historical case studies offer valuable insights into how vice presidential picks have shaped past elections. Examples such as Lyndon B. Johnson's impact on Kennedy's 1960 campaign and George H. W. Bush's role in Reagan's 1980 victory illustrates the strategic importance of selecting a running mate who can balance the ticket, appeal to key demographics, and influence swing states. These case studies underscore the potential for Shapiro's candidacy to impact the 2024 election in similar ways.

Strategies for Republicans Moving Forward

In response to Shapiro's potential influence, Republicans are refining their strategies. Key tactics include emphasising economic issues, presenting alternative healthcare solutions, and highlighting their own policy achievements. Building strong alliances, targeting swing voters, and preparing for debates and media appearances are also crucial. Republicans aim to counter Shapiro's appeal and mobilise their base to maintain competitiveness in the evolving electoral landscape.

The Role of Social Media

Social media will play a critical role in shaping perceptions of Shapiro and the broader election dynamics. Both parties are leveraging social media platforms to promote their messages, engage with voters, and counteract opposing narratives. Shapiro's presence on the ticket may influence social media discussions and trends, impacting public opinion and voter engagement too. Effective social media strategies will be essential for both Democrats and Republicans as they navigate the complexities of the 2024 election.

This bonus chapter provides a comprehensive look at the insights and analyses surrounding Josh Shapiro's potential impact on the 2024 election. Expert commentary, Republican strategists' views, media analysis, and polling data offer a multifaceted perspective on Shapiro's role and influence.

Understanding these factors is crucial for navigating the evolving political landscape and preparing for the challenges and opportunities of the upcoming election.

THANK YOU!

Thank you for choosing to read this book. Your support and curiosity drive the pursuit of knowledge and understanding in our ever-evolving political landscape. It's readers like you who make the effort to explore complex issues and engage in thoughtful discourse.

I deeply appreciate your investment in this journey with me, and I hope this book provides valuable insights and enhances your understanding of the critical topics discussed. Your engagement is vital to the ongoing dialogue that shapes the future of the Americans.

Leaving a review is simple and only takes a few minutes. Your support and feedback are greatly appreciated.

Thank you once again for your time and interest.

With sincere appreciation,

JIM K. CLARK.

www.ingramcontent.com/pod-product-compliance
Lightning Source LLC
Chambersburg PA
CBHW051711250726
48653CB00007B/2964